At the Butterfly Conservatory

Represent and Interpret Data

Ron Royce

INFOMAX MATH READERS

Rosen Classroom™

New York

Published in 2015 by The Rosen Publishing Group, Inc.
29 East 21st Street, New York, NY 10010

Book Design: Katelyn Londino

Photo Credits: Cover Rich Reid/National Geographic/Getty Images; pp. 3–24 (sky background) Grisha Bruev/
Shutterstock.com; pp. 3–24 (vector design background) tatkuptsova/Shutterstock.com; p. 5 http://en.wikipedia.org/wiki/
File:Day_Butterfly_Center.jpg/Wikipedia.org; pp. 7, 9, 11, 13, 15, 17, 19 (ruler) SmileStudio/Shutterstock.com;
p. 7 Aleksandr Morozov/Flickr Open/Getty Images; p. 9 AlessandroZocc/Shutterstock.com; p. 11 somyot pattana/
Shutterstock.com; p. 13 Ksenia Ragozina/Shutterstock.com; p. 15 (butterfly) Shutterschock/Shutterstock.com;
p. 15 (leaf background) somchaij/Shutterstock.com; p. 17 David Kay/Shutterstock.com; p. 19 (main) Leena Robinson/
Shutterstock.com; p. 19 (inset) Chris Hill/Shutterstock.com; p. 21 Sari ONeal/Shutterstock.com; p. 22 kostrez/
Shutterstock.com.

ISBN: 978-1-4777-4597-7
6-pack ISBN: 978-1-4777-4599-1

Manufactured in the United States of America

CPSIA Compliance Information: Batch #WS15RC: For further information contact Rosen Publishing, New York, New York at 1-800-237-9932.

Contents

The Wonderful Natural World

Alexis loves to learn about nature. Her favorite subject is science. In science class, Alexis learns about all the wonderful plants and animals in the world around us. She especially likes to learn about **insects**.

This year, Alexis's class is learning about butterflies. Alexis sometimes sees butterflies in her neighborhood, but she's only seen a few. That's going to change this year, though, because Alexis's class is going on a field trip to her city's butterfly conservatory. It's a zoo just for butterflies!

People visit butterfly conservatories to see different **species** of butterflies and learn how they live and grow.

The field trip will be fun, but it's also a chance to learn important facts about butterflies, such as what they look like and how big they are.

To really understand the basics of butterflies, Alexis's class will take measurements of the different objects they see in the butterfly conservatory. Alexis's teacher says it's very important to take exact measurements because they provide the most correct information about the species. Alexis will use her ruler to take exact measurements of objects around the butterfly conservatory.

A ruler has marks for inches, half inches, and quarter inches. An inch is 1 whole. A half inch is 1 of 2 equal parts a whole inch is divided into. A quarter inch, also called a fourth inch, is 1 of 4 equal parts a whole inch is divided into.

1 inch

half inch

fourth inch

inches   1   2   3   4   5

The Butterfly's Life Cycle

Alexis's class walks through the conservatory with a guide who explains everything they see around them. He says the plants and flowers are like those in a butterfly's natural **habitat**.

The guide explains the steps of a butterfly's life. It begins as an egg, grows into a caterpillar, then becomes a butterfly. The change from a caterpillar to butterfly is called metamorphosis (meh-tuh-MOHR-fuh-suhs). Alexis sees a leaf with many butterfly eggs. They're too small for her to measure each one, but she can measure the entire group.

Alexis lines up one edge of the eggs with the first mark on the ruler. She looks at the place on the ruler where the group of eggs ends. It reaches the 1-inch mark. This group of eggs measures 1 whole inch.

Alexis's class moves to another area of the conservatory. Here, they see caterpillars. Caterpillars hatch from eggs like the ones Alexis just saw. They spend most of their time eating leaves and gaining weight.

Alexis sees a caterpillar creeping along a leaf nearby. She lines up her ruler with the caterpillar's body. She sees the 1-inch mark, but the caterpillar's body is longer than that. It's longer than the next fourth-inch mark, too. It stops at the next half-inch mark. This caterpillar is exactly $1\frac{1}{2}$ inches long.

> This caterpillar's body takes up 1 whole inch and 1 half of the next inch on the ruler. Alexis knows the caterpillar is $1\frac{1}{2}$ inches long.

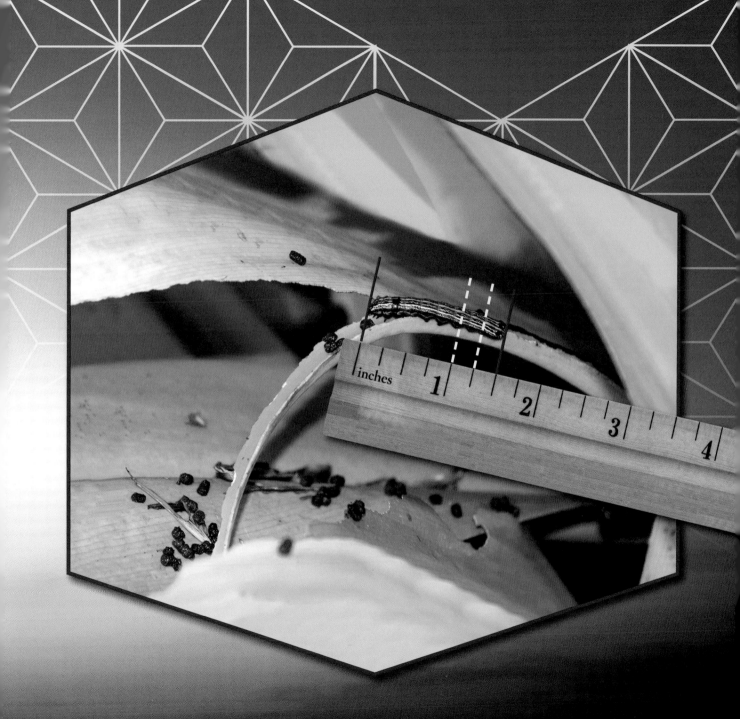

Next, the guide teaches Alexis's class something really cool. He says the next stage of a butterfly's life is the pupa (PYOO-puh) stage. It begins when a caterpillar spins silk around its body and forms a chrysalis (KRIH-suh-luhs), which is a hard outer casing that protects its body. Inside the chrysalis, the caterpillar changes into a beautiful butterfly.

Alexis sees a chrysalis hanging from a branch. It's too **delicate** to touch, so Alexis has to hold the ruler a little bit away from the chrysalis. How long is it?

This chrysalis goes as far as 3 short marks on the ruler. The marks each **represent** $\frac{1}{4}$ of an inch. Together, they're 3 of 4 equal parts of an inch. That means this chrysalis is $\frac{3}{4}$ of an inch long.

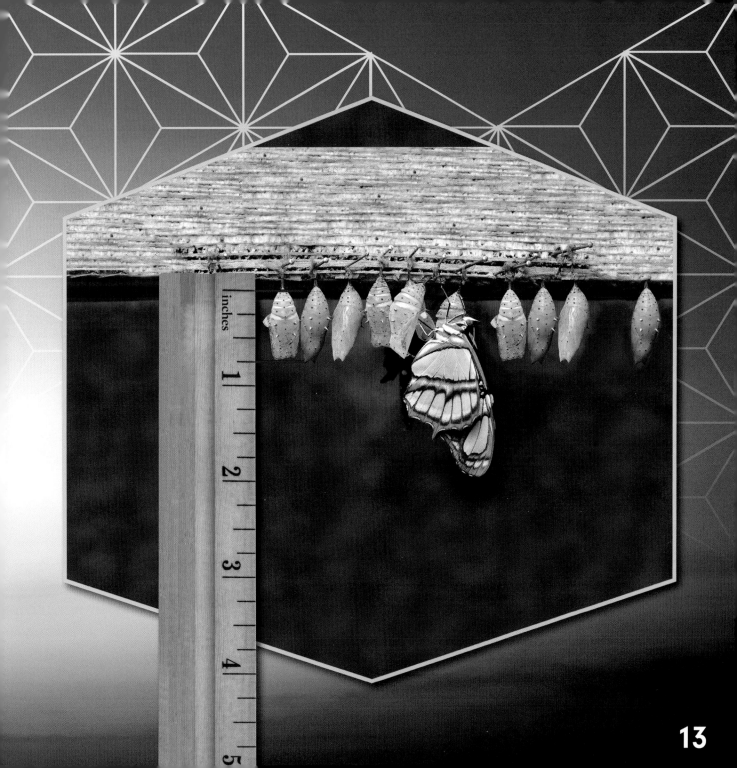

Beautiful Butterflies

It's finally time for the class to see the best part of the butterfly conservatory—the butterflies! There are butterflies of many different sizes and colors flying around. The first butterfly Alexis sees is a kind she's seen in her yard before. It's the painted lady butterfly.

The guide points to a painted lady butterfly that has landed on a leaf. He says this butterfly has a **wingspan** of $2\frac{1}{2}$ inches. Alexis finds that measurement on her ruler by counting 2 whole-inch marks. Then she finds the half-inch mark past the 2-inch mark.

> The guide says the butterfly's colors come from the scales that cover its wings. Each scale is one color. Together, they make the wings look beautiful.

The butterfly conservatory has large, flowering plants. Alexis learns the butterflies feed on the nectar, or sweet juice, inside the flowers. While she's looking at a group of orange flowers, a black-and-white striped butterfly lands on them to feed. It's the zebra swallowtail butterfly.

Alexis gently holds her ruler up in front of the butterfly. It stays there long enough for her to measure its wingspan, which she sees is $3\frac{1}{4}$ inches. That measurement can be thought of as 3 whole inches plus a quarter of another inch.

This butterfly landed on the flower to feed. Sometimes a butterfly will land on a person who's wearing a brightly colored shirt. The color makes the butterfly think it's landing on a flower.

Next, Alexis sees a butterfly with beautifully shaped wings. The guide says it's the question mark butterfly. The name comes from a silver mark on the underside of its wings that looks like a question mark.

The question mark butterfly's wingspan is shown on this ruler. Alexis thinks this measurement looks familiar. That's because this butterfly has the same size wingspan as the zebra swallowtail butterfly. Its wingspan is $3\frac{1}{4}$ inches long, too. Even though these 2 butterflies belong to different species, they have something in common.

This question mark butterfly's wingspan ends at the first quarter-inch mark between the 3-inch and 4-inch marks on Alexis's ruler. Alexis knows this means the wingspan measures $3\frac{1}{4}$ inches.

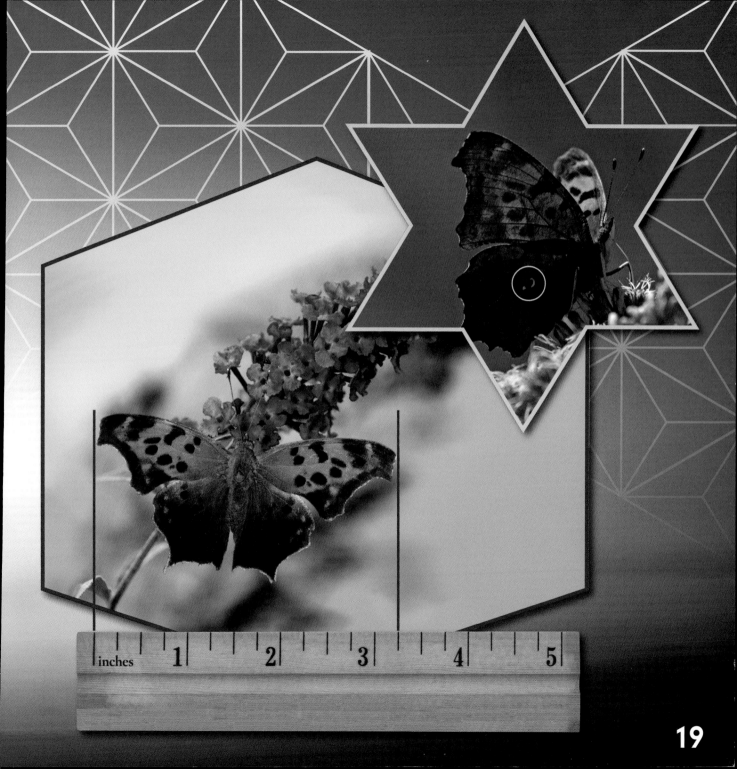

Graphing the Measurements

Soon, it's time for Alexis's class to leave the butterfly conservatory. Alexis's teacher says they'll use the measurements they took on the field trip to make a line plot. A line plot is a **graph** that shows how often something occurs.

Alexis's line plot shows quarter-inch, half-inch, and whole-inch measurements. She puts an X above a measurement if she measured something of that size while at the butterfly conservatory. What does the **data** on Alexis's line plot show about her measurements?

This data shows that Alexis took 6 different measurements. There are 2 Xs above the $3\frac{1}{4}$-inch mark, which means she took this measurement twice.

Measurements at the Conservatory

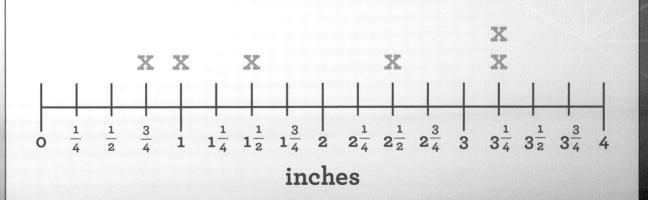

inches

x = measurement

Alexis's Butterfly Garden

Alexis loved going to the butterfly conservatory. In fact, it was her favorite field trip she's ever taken with her school. She learned many interesting facts about butterflies. She even learned about how to make a garden that will bring butterflies to her very own backyard.

Alexis is going to make a butterfly garden this spring. Planting lots of beautiful, colorful flowers will attract many different kinds of butterflies. Alexis may even try to measure them. It's a great way to learn about just one thing that makes butterflies special!

Glossary

data (DAY-tuh) Facts and figures.

delicate (DEH-lih-kuht) Requiring careful handling.

graph (GRAAF) A chart showing the relationship between two things.

habitat (HAA-buh-tat) An animal, plant, or other organism's natural home.

insect (IHN-sehkt) A bug.

represent (reh-prih-ZEHNT) To stand for.

species (SPEE-sheez) A group of living things that are all the same kind.

wingspan (WING-spaan) The measurement from the tip of 1 wing to the tip of the other.

Index